A CHAIN OF EVENTS

SEASIDE AND WAYSIDE

BOOK ONE

by

Julia McNair Wright

Then Nature, the old nurse, took
The child upon her knee,
Saying, "Here is a story-book
Thy Father hath written for thee."
— LONGFELLOW *to* AGASSIZ

YESTERDAY'S CLASSICS

ITHACA, NEW YORK

This edition, first published in 2022 by Yesterday's Classics, an imprint of Yesterday's Classics, LLC, is an unabridged republication of the text originally published by D. C. Heath & Co. in 1903. For the complete listing of the books that are published by Yesterday's Classics, please visit www.yesterdaysclassics.com. Yesterday's Classics is the publishing arm of Gateway to the Classics which presents the complete text of hundreds of classic books for children at www.gatewaytoclassics.com.

ISBN: 978-1-63334-074-9

Yesterday's Classics, LLC
PO Box 339
Ithaca, NY 14851

PREFACE

THIS series of Nature Readers is intended for the use of beginners in reading. The subjects chosen and their treatment have been alike subordinated to this object. The Nature Readers are not offered as text-books in natural science, but rather as a contribution to the idea that facts of real and permanent value may be made known, a noble taste may be cultivated, thought may be developed, and the initiatory steps in an increasingly popular study may be taken, while a child is learning to read a certain number of English words.

Should not the first short, strong Saxon sentences be used to convey scientific facts rather than such trivial information as,

"The boy has a new hat," or, "I had a plate of green corn to eat on the fourth day of July"?

Lessons fresh from the seashore and the field, where life is seen, not in an abnormal state, as captivity, but in its own chosen homes and natural development, cannot fail to have an educative power of great value, even to minds of a very early age.

The real difficulty to be overcome has been to put these simple lessons concerning the habits, homes, and anatomy of certain animals into such words as are usually found in the most elementary reading-books. To accomplish this, so that the series shall reach the hands for which it was intended, has been the author's chief concern. There is happily no uncertainty as to the scientific accuracy of the work. Every substantive statement has been verified by the observation of the author, or of those whose competency for such work is unquestioned. The practical value of this series of Nature Readers must now be tried in the homes and the schools.

Whether the pages have been discreetly broken into paragraphs to catch restless and unaccustomed eyes, whether the words and subjects have been fitly chosen, whether the individuality and personality given to irrational animals shall succeed in attracting the interest and fixing the wandering thought of childhood, are all questions rather to be answered by a trial of the book than argued in a preface.

We bring no cat and dog stories, no tales of monkey antics; but we have endeavored to impress upon the little heir of life, in one of its highest forms, a comprehension of life, and a reverence for it, even in some of its lower manifestations.

This object has already been kindly commended and generously welcomed by no small number of skilled teachers and scientists, who have given valuable time to the reading of manuscript and proof of this series.

To those parents and teachers who will give the books a careful trial, and reinforce these simple instructions by their own enthusiasm and experience, the Nature Readers are commended by

THE AUTHOR.

TO THE BOYS AND GIRLS

Do you know that there are cities on your path to school, and under the trees in your garden? Do you know that homes with many rooms in them hang in the branches above your head? Do you know that what you call "little bugs" hunt and fish, make paper, saw wood, are masons and weavers, and feed and guard and teach their little ones, much as your papa and mamma take care of you? This sounds like a fairy story, but it is a true fairy story.

In this book you will read of some of these wonders. And when you have read this book well, you shall have two or three more.

These books will not try to tell you all that there is to tell of these things. They are only to wake up your minds, so that you will think and study and notice these things for yourselves.

Your eyes will be worth many times as much to you as they now are, when you learn to observe with care and to think about what you see.

J. M. N. W.

CONTENTS

Mr. Crab

LESSON I

MR. AND MRS. CRAB

This is a picture of Mr. Crab. He lives in the sand by the seaside.

Mr. Crab has a smooth, flat shell on his back. He has eight legs and two hands.

One hand is large; the other hand is small. He fights with the big hand, and takes his food with the little hand, or with both hands.

Mr. Crab digs out his house in the sand. He makes a place for a hall, a bed-room, and a pantry.

1

Do you see the round hole? It is the doorway of his house.

Mrs. Crab

Mrs. Crab does not dig. Both her hands are small and weak. She gets food to put into the pantry.

She never fights. If she is in any trouble she runs home, or to a hole in a rock.

See what queer eyes! They are set on pegs; some call them stalks. The crab can push out the eye-pegs and pull them in.

Would you not look odd if you could make your eyes stand out six inches?

When crabs go into their houses, they draw down their eyes and tuck in their feet.

Crabs are of many colors. They are red, brown, green, yellow, and blue. The claws are often of a very bright color.

The color on the shell is less bright than on the claws; it is in small dots. The color on some kinds of crabs is in lines.

No crab is clear, bright red when it is alive. When it is boiled it takes a fine, red hue. Why this is no one can tell.

LESSON II

MR. CRAB AND HIS HOUSE

THE water of the sea comes and goes in tides.

The water rises twice each day.—That is high tide. The water goes back after each high tide.—That is ebb tide. Each tide lasts six hours.

When the snow melts in the spring, or when much rain falls, the water rises high in the brook. In the dry, hot days the water is low in the bed of the stream.

If the stream or brook were full and low twice each day, the change would be like the high and low tides of the sea.

When the tide is low, Mr. Crab digs out his house. He scoops out the sand with his big claw. Then he folds his claw to carry the sand, as you can carry grass or leaves on your arm. Some kinds of crabs carry the sand in three of their feet, bent to form a basket.

Mr. Crab makes his House.

Mr. Crab takes the sand to the top of his hole. Then, with a jerk, he throws the sand into a heap.

Mr. Crab is very strong. He can lift and carry things larger than his body.

He digs out a long hall. He makes rooms in his house.

Then he goes with his wife to look for food. They keep near their home.

Crabs eat flies, gnats, ants, lady-birds, and other little insects. They eat seaweed also.

When beach-flies light on the sand or on seaweed, the crabs jump at them, and catch them as cats catch mice.

But the cats do not move so quickly as the crabs.

Mr. and Mrs. Crab put the bugs they catch into their pantry.

For six hours, while the tide is high, they stay in their house; and while they stay in the house they eat insects and seaweed they have stored away.

Mr. Crab acts as though he knew about the tide. He knows when it will be high over his house. He knows when it will be low, so that he can come out.

LESSON III

MORE ABOUT MR. CRAB

I⊤ would take a year to tell all the odd things about Mr. Crab.

Where are your bones? They are inside your body. Your bones are a frame to hold up your soft flesh.

Mr. Crab's bones are on the outside of his body. His bones are his armor, to keep him from being hurt.

Look at his hard shell, he has no other bones.

He can both walk and swim. You can live only on land. The crab can live and breathe either in water or on land.

Mrs. Crab lays eggs. A hen, you know, lays eggs, one by one, in a nest. She keeps them warm till the chicks come out.

The crab's eggs are put in a long tube or sack. Mrs. Crab does not leave them in a nest. She carries them tied on her legs, or under her body.

When the small crabs come out of the eggs, they grow very fast.

When you catch a crab by his arm or leg, he will pinch you, if he can, with his big claw. If you do not let go, he drops off this arm or leg, and runs.

Mr. Crab runs away.

Could you run with one leg gone? The crab has legs to spare. Then, too, his legs will grow again. Yours would not.

A crab's leg, or hand, will grow again very soon, when one has been lost.

If his eye-peg is cut off, it takes a whole year for a new eye to grow. I think he knows that; he is very careful of his eyes.

The eye-pegs of one kind of crab are very long. He has a wide, flat shell. There is a notch in each side of his shell. He can let his eyes lie in that notch.[1]

How can he do that? His eye-pegs are so long that he can bend them down flat to the shell and keep them safe in the notch.

LESSON IV

MR. AND MRS. CRAB GET A NEW COAT

YOUR skin is soft and fine. As you grow more and more, your skin does not break. Your skin gets larger as your body grows.

Mr. Crab is in a hard shell. The shell will not stretch. It gets too tight, and what can Mr. Crab do then?

[1] See picture in Lesson IX.

What do you do when your coat is too small?

Now I will tell you a strange thing. When Mr. Crab finds that his shell is too small, he takes it off, as you take off your coat.

He pulls his legs, his hands, and his back, out of his shell. He does that in his house in the sand.

Spider Crab

You do not undress out of doors. You go to your room. So does Mr. Crab.

Mr. Crab slips out of his shell. He pulls out his feet and hands, as if he took off his boots and his gloves. Then he is a poor, soft, cold thing. But over all his body is spread a skin, soft as paste, like glue and lime. In a few days it gets hard. It is as big as Mr. Crab, and just fits his shape. Here is a good, new shell!

Little Pinna Crab

When crabs get new shells we say they moult. This shell has the right colors—blue, brown, red, or gold. It has spots and rings.

When Mrs. Crab changes her shell, Mr. Crab stays near and tries to keep her from being hurt.

The young crabs have to change their shells often, they grow so fast.

Crabs that live in dark mud have dark brown or green shells.

Some crabs have sand-colored shells[2]— pale gray or brown shells, with close, fine specks like sand on them.

There are more kinds of crabs than you could count. They live in all parts of the world. This book tells you of only a few of them.

LESSON V

WHAT THE CRAB DOES

THE crab is quick to get cross. Are you? He likes to fight. In that he is like a bad boy.

When Mr. Crab sees some other crab near his house, he is angry.

Then he stands high on his toes. He pulls in his eye-pegs, for fear they will be hurt. He spreads out his big arm. Now he is ready to fight!

He runs at his enemy! Each tries to hit

[2] See Lesson XXXIII.

the other with his big claw. This big claw, or hand, can cut and pinch hard.

Sometimes one crab cuts off the hand or leg of the other crab. Or he bites the shell on his back.

Sometimes you may find on the beach crab shells with the scars of these bites or cuts.

If only a leg is cut off, the crab may keep on fighting. But if his hand, or eye, or back shell is hurt, he can fight no more.

He runs home to hide, until a new eye, or hand, or leg can grow. If your hand is cut off, will it grow again? No, it will not.

When Mr. Crab has lost a leg or hand, and a new one grows, it is small at first. When he gets a new coat, the new hand or leg becomes half as large as the one he lost.

With the next new coat, the new hand or leg comes out the full size it should be.

When a crab is afraid, he runs home. He is very brave, and does not much fear other crabs.

He fears birds most; for birds eat small crabs; and the crab cannot fight a big bird.

Swing a rag over a crab's head. What does he do? Up fly his eye-pegs! Up comes his big hand! There, he has caught the rag!

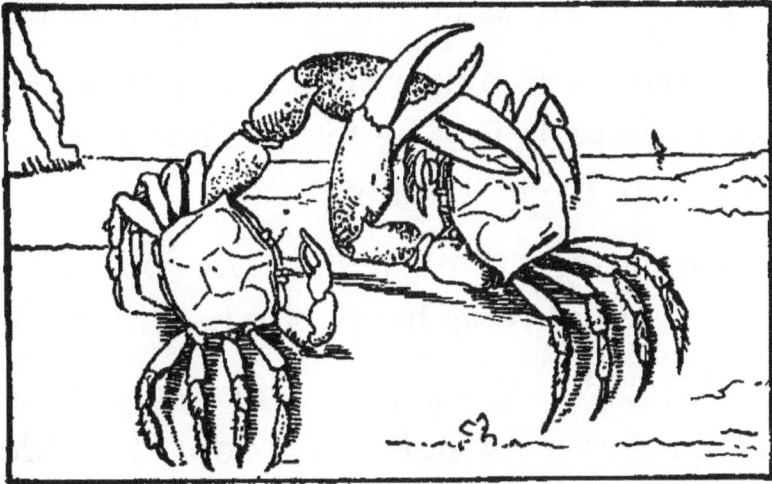

A Free Fight

He will not let go. You can lift him into the air by the rag; still he holds on.

Once I saw a blue crab catch a dog's tail. The crab held on fast. The dog yelped, and ran up and down the beach. We had to catch the dog, and pry open the crab's claw.

Let us look at this crab; he has let go the rag, and has gone to dig in his house. Lay this bit of shell on his hole. See it shake! He has run up and hit it with his head.

Now he waits. Watch well. What will Mr. Crab do next?

There, the shell flies up in the air! He struck it hard as he ran, and made it fly up.

I have seen him try twice, and make the shell shake before he found how hard he must hit, to get it out of the way.

Some folks think he shuts the door of his house with his big hand. I do not think so.

He knows that the tide will wash a lump of sand over his hole, for a door. The tide shuts him in.

The crab watches the waves come nearer as the tide rises. At last he jumps through his doorway, for he knows that the next wave will close it.

He never stays up one wave too long. He gets in in time. He is shut in his house with Mrs. Crab. He knows that the tide will pass, and he has bugs to eat.

LESSON VI

MR. CRAB AND HIS FRIENDS

THE crab that has one large claw has many names. Some call him the Fighting Crab, he is so cross.

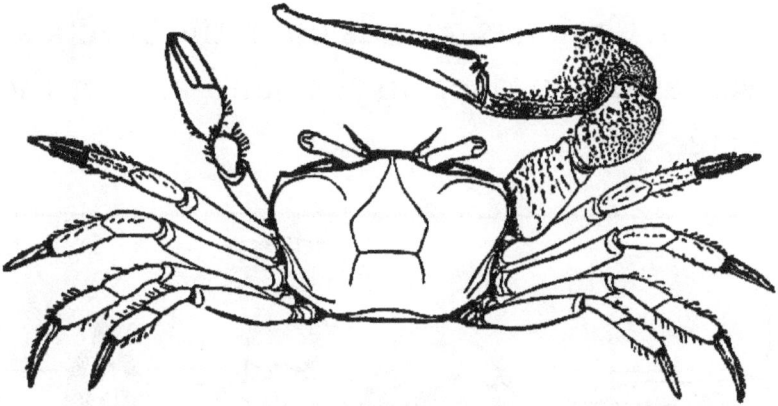

The Fiddler Crab

Others name him the Calling Crab, because, when he runs, he holds his big claw high, as if he called, "Come! come!"

Most people call him the Fiddler Crab, and say that his big claw is his fiddle.

I think Fiddler Crab is the best name for him. He can, and does, play a tune on that hand. It is his violin, as well as his hand, his spade, and his sword.

Do you see a row of little knobs on the inner edge of his big claw? He rubs those knobs on the edge of the shell that covers his back, and the sound is his tune.

He uses that tune to call his mate. Mrs. Crab thinks it is a fine tune.

Mr. Crab has friends upon the beach, as well as down deep in the sand and in the water.

Mr. Crab and Some of His Friends

When he walks along the sand, he meets big flies with two wings. He is glad to see them. Why? They put their grubs, or young ones, in the sand, and Mr. Crab knows that he can find them to eat.

Mr. Crab also meets a great, green tiger beetle. He does not fight with him. He knows that he shall find the beetle's grubs in the sand and eat them.

More Friends of Mr. Crab

While he is digging down below, he meets a little fat, round crab, with big eyes, and a thin, gray shell. He is glad to see him.

If Mr. Crab has not food enough to eat while the tide is high, he will creep along in the sand, and catch and kill this small crab for his dinner.

Mr. Crab also meets, deep down in the sand, long, green, red, or brown worms. They are making houses for themselves. He does not trouble them.

Out in the sea, Mr. Crab finds some small shell-fish called limpets. He likes them so much that he lets them live on his shell. They take fast hold on his back, and he does not pull them off.

LESSON VII

SOME OTHER CRABS[3]

ALL crabs are not alike. There are many kinds. They differ in shape, color, and habits.

Some are not at all pretty. Some are very pretty. All are very strange.

The Spider Crab[4] has long, thin legs. The front of his shell, which is over his head, is not wide, but is a sharp point. This is to help him dig his way into sand and mud.

---

[3] See illustrations on pages 2, 9, 10, and 21.

[4] See picture in Lesson IV.

Some crabs do not make a house in the sand; they live in holes in the rocks.

The Horse-Shoe Crab is of a chestnut color.

Some call him the King Crab. Look at his picture. His shell is of the shape of the hoof of a horse, but it has a long tail, with sharp points on the edges. The tail is as hard as wood, and has edges like a file.

The Horse-Shoe or King Crab lives in sand and in mud. He chooses the muddy banks where rivers or streams run into the sea. He pushes his way in the mud, with his big, round shell, and scrapes the mud out with his many feet. He eats the worms he finds in the sand and mud.

Why are the worms down there? Like Mr. Crab, they build a house in the mud. Some time I will tell you about these worms.

Now and then, as Mr. Crab goes along under the ground, he finds in his way a long, soft thing that looks good to eat. It is the long pipe or tube with which a clam takes his food. The King Crab puts out his claw to get it. The King Crab can move his hand claw as quickly as your cat can strike with her paw. But the clam is far more quick than the King Crab, and shuts his shell down on the King Crab's claw. Now is he held fast, like a rat in a trap!

The King Crab waits to see if the clam will let go. No, he will not. Then the crab drops off his claw, and goes away to hide while a new one grows.

Do you see, in the picture, a crab in a shell made like a curl? That crab steals his house. He finds an empty shell, and goes into it to live. It is odd to see him run, with the shell he stole on his back.

How does this crab live? By fishing. All crabs hunt and fish. I have told you how they hunt on the sand for bugs and flies. Did I not tell you how they hunt for grubs and worms under ground?

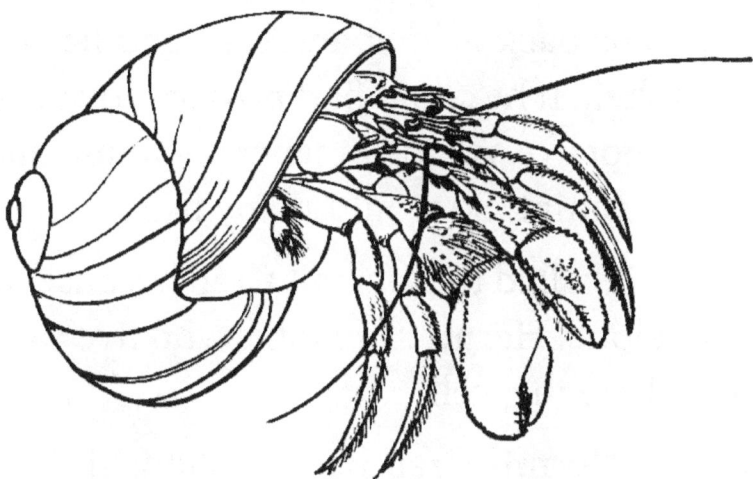

The House He Lives In

How do crabs fish? Mr. Crab gets into a good place to fish. He pops out his eyes to see all about him. Then when things that he likes to eat float by, he strikes out with his big hand.

He catches what he wants nearly every time, he is so quick. Crabs are very greedy; they spend much time eating.

LESSON VIII

THE HERMIT CRAB

Do you wish to hear more about the crab that steals his house? Why does he do that? His back is long and soft, and has no hard shell. If he could find no hard cover, he could not live. All the other crabs would bite or pinch him. So would many fish.

He is called the Hermit Crab because he lives alone. Hermits are folks who live each one alone in a cell.

The Hermit Crab has no one with him in his shell.

He has company not far off.

Great numbers of these crabs may be seen creeping about together.

As the Hermit Crab grows too big for one shell, he finds another. He never stays outside his shell until he knows that he is about to die. How does he know that? I cannot tell.

He comes out, lies flat down by his house,

and dies. He wants his house to live in, not to die in.

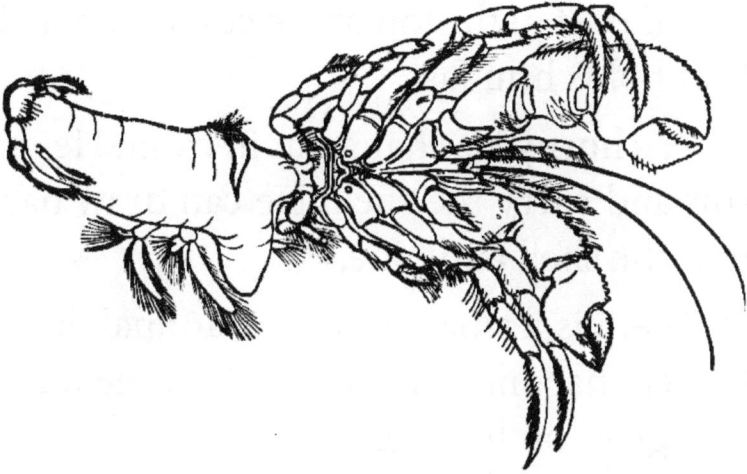

He comes out to die.

When he needs to change his shell-house, he hunts for one to suit him. Then he puts in his long claw, to feel if it is clean and empty. Now and then he finds another crab in it. Then the two fight for it.

If some small thing lives in the shell which the hermit wants, he pulls it out with his long claw. Then he brings the new shell near, and springs from the shell he is in to the shell he wants, as you would spring from chair to chair.

On the end of his long, soft tail he has a hook. He twists his soft body into the new shell. Then he clasps his tail-hook to a small, round post in the top of the curl of the shell. That holds him fast.

His horny legs hang out in front. He can run and carry the shell. He can draw back into the shell and hide.

There is a small, pink sea-animal, like a flower, that one kind of crab likes. He wants it to grow on his shell.

It may be that it helps him to catch food. It may be that he likes it to hide the door of his shell.

Why? Perhaps that he may be hidden as he fishes for his dinner. You know hunters and fishers hide sometimes so that their prey will come nearer to them.

This pink sea-creature can build more shell on the edge of the one the crab lives in. This makes the shell larger. Then the crab need not move so often.

When he moves, he takes his friend with

him. He puts out his claw and lifts her off his old shell, and sets her on the edge of the new one. Then he holds her there until she has made herself fast. Then he slips in, tail first.

The fine red, pink, and white frills of the friend hang like a veil over his door. They keep fish and other foes away. For this pink thing can sting.

Once I found a nice shell. I thought it was empty, and I kept it for eight or ten days in a box. Then I laid it on a shelf. One day I heard, clack! clack! clack! And there was my shell running up and down the shelf! I was in a tent close by the sea. I do not know when that animal got into that shell.

In the South Seas some of these crabs do not live in sea shells. They live in cocoa-nut shells. They eat the meat of the nuts. When all of it is eaten they seek for another shell.

Each night these crabs crawl into the water to get wet. They leave their eggs in the water to hatch.

LESSON IX

THE CRAB'S ENEMIES

CRABS have many enemies. Fish and birds eat crabs. Men eat some kinds of crabs. Crabs eat each other.

His home is on the sea.

With so many enemies, soon no crabs would be left if they did not lay so many eggs. Mrs. Crab, each year, lays more eggs than you could count.

Crabs do not always have hard shells. When they first come from the egg they have long tails, four legs, and no claws. The crab's body then has a thin cover.

At this time of his life he is very helpless, like a baby. He can swim well, and so can escape some of his enemies. When he gets claws and a hard shell, he is safer.

A little pink crab, named Pea Crab, or Pinna Crab, goes to live in the shell of the oyster. The oyster does not seem to mind it. You may see this little crab in your oyster soup. He turns orange color when he is cooked. The Pinna, or Pea Crab, has a very soft shell.

The Spider Crab has a brown shell, rough like sand. Little thorns grow all over it. The Spider Crab cuts off fine seaweed with her little sharp claws, and hangs it like ribbons on these thorns or hooks.[5] Then she looks like a little green grove! Who can tell why she does that? Is it to hide?

Do you see the wide hind feet of the crab in this picture?

[5] See picture in Lesson IV.

Those are his paddles, or oars. They are his swimming feet. His shell is wide and light. He can float on the waves like a boat. He goes far out on the sea.

Some crabs can dig into the sand very fast. They go in backwards. They slip out of sight like a flash. Or, they leave out the tips of their heads and their eye-pegs, to look about.

Sand Crabs do this.

The shells of Sand Crabs are a pale brown or sand color. These shells are wide and round behind, and come to a point in the front. They are very rough. The crabs' heads are in the narrow part of the shell. Sand Crabs are swift runners.

Some crabs hide in holes in the rocks. Often their color protects them. When they are afraid, they lie flat on the sand, and it is hard to see them. Some birds have long, thin bills, with which to pick Mr. Crab out of his sand house.

LESSON X

THE USES OF CRABS

How often does Mr. Crab need a new coat? His coat does not wear out, but it becomes too small. Then he changes it for a larger one. He cannot stretch it or piece it.

The baby grows fast. You can almost see it grow. You grow fast. They say it is hard to keep you in clothes. You cannot wear the coat you had last year.

Your papa can wear his coat for many years. He will tell you that he has stopped growing.

It is so with the crab. When he is young, he grows fast. He needs a new shell very often. When he is older, he grows more slowly. Then he gets a new coat every spring.

At last he does not grow any more. He keeps the same shell,[6] year after year. It gets very hard and thick, and loses its bright color.

[6] The large claw may be on either the right or left side of the crab.

Very often it is nearly covered with limpets. They fasten their flat or pointed shells to the crab's back, and stay there.

I cannot tell you just how long a crab lives. Some of them look very old.

Of what use is a crab? Have all things a use? Yes. God made all things; and all things are of use. Sometimes we cannot find out the use.

Crabs are good for food. Some kinds are eaten by men, as fish and oysters are eaten. Birds eat a great many crabs. Some birds almost live on them. Fish eat many crabs. There are many kinds of crabs so small that you could hardly see them. Fish feed on them.

Crabs help to keep the sea and the seashore clean. That makes it pleasant and healthful.

Crabs are greedy. They eat nearly all kinds of dead things that would spoil and make a bad smell if left on the sand.

They eat dead fish, dead animals that are thrown into the sea, and grubs, flies, and

Mr. Crab has a Picnic.

worms. Do you ever see men going about to clean the streets? Crabs in their way do such work as these men.

The crabs help to keep clean the sea as well as the shore. There are so many crabs, and they eat so much, and so fast, that they can clean away much of the dead stuff that lies on the shore, or near it at low tide.

LESSON XI

MRS. WASP AND HER HOME

HERE is a round hole on the hill-side path. Is it a crab's hole?

A Wayside Home

No, it is too far from the sea for a crab. Mrs. Wasp made it for her baby to live in.

Her name is Vespa. In her house she has a hall, a room, and a bed. In the bed her baby lies asleep. It is now a soft, white egg.

When the baby wasp comes out of the egg, he will be all alone. When Mrs. Wasp has laid the egg safe in bed, she goes away.

She shuts her door with a lump of mud. She leaves her baby some food to eat. The food is a pile of little caterpillars. When she leaves her baby, she never comes back.

When he gets big, he digs his way out, and off he flies. If he meets his mother he does not know her.

Mrs. Wasp makes her bed of fine sawdust. She cuts the wood up soft and fine. She has two small, sharp saws with which to do this.

She can make paper out of wood. How does she do that? She saws the wood into a fine dust. Then she mixes it with glue from her mouth. When she takes it home, she spreads it out thin with her feet.

It dries into fine, gray paper. With it she papers her house, to keep her baby warm and dry.

Mrs. Wasp is cross, but she is wise. She has a long sting. She kills, or puts into a deep sleep, the caterpillars that she takes home. This keeps them from decay.

She is never idle, she has so much to

do making and furnishing her house, and storing up food.

The wasp in the picture is called the Hermit Wasp, because she lives alone.

LESSON XII

WHAT MRS. WASP CAN DO

How does Mrs. Wasp make paper? First she finds a piece of dry, old wood.

She cuts off bits of wood, like fine, soft threads. She wets these with a kind of glue from her mouth, and rolls them into a ball.

Then, she stands on her hind legs, and with her front feet puts the ball between her jaws.

She then flies to her nest.

She uses her tongue, her jaws, and her feet, to spread the ball out thin. On her hind legs she has flat feet, to help her lay down the paper.

She lays one sheet of paper on the other,

until it is thick enough to make a nest. Some wasps hang these paper nests in trees.

The nests are round, like balls, or they may be the shape of a top. At the bottom of each you will find two doors.

The wasp that builds in a tree does not live alone.

She has in her home very many paper rooms. They are like cells in a honey-comb. Sometimes she lays one sheet of her paper upon another until it is strong paste-board.

She can make wax. She puts a wax lid on the cells.

She can make varnish, to keep the cells dry.

A Paper House

35

One kind of wasp is a mason.

Her house is made of mud. She brings mud in little balls, and builds a house.

In the house she puts a baby wasp. She puts in little spiders for him to eat.

A hornet is a kind of wasp. We may call him Mrs. Wasp's cousin. Hornets catch and eat flies.

There is a black wasp that is called a mud-dauber. She builds a little mud house. I know a boy who broke one of these mud houses thirty-two times.

The wasp built it up each time. One of these mud-wasps built a house ten times on a man's desk. Each time that he broke it up, she built it again.

This kind of wasp does not leave her baby alone. She waits until it is hatched from the egg, and then she feeds and cares for it.

LESSON XIII

A LOOK AT MRS. WASP

Mrs. Wasp's color is blue-black. She has yellow marks.

She has four thin wings. Two are large and two are small.

The front wings are the large ones. Her wings lie close to her sides when her body is at rest.

The wasp looks as if she had two wings, not four.

The two under ones are hooked to the upper ones.

Mrs. Wasp

Her eyes are set close to her head. They are large.

They have a notch or dent in them. She has two long wands, called feelers, on her head. They are made in joints. She touches things with them.

Her body is in three parts. The first part is the head, with the eyes and mouth.

The next part is thick and short. The hind part is long and slim. These two join at a point. It looks as if the hind part might drop off, but it never does.

Mrs. Wasp has a long, sharp sting in her tail. The wasp's sting is like two fine saws. A drop of poison runs through it from a bag.

You need not fear Mrs. Wasp. She does not sting if you let her alone.

She has six legs. The legs and wings are set on the part of the body that is next the head.

She uses her front legs for hands. The body of the wasp is hard, and made of rings like scales.

Mrs. Wasp uses her jaws to cut up wood for paper. She does not need them to eat with.

She eats honey. When her baby eats spiders and caterpillars, it does not chew them. It sucks out their juice. People say that wasps bite fruit and spoil it. That is when they make a hole in the fruit to suck out the juice. Wasps kill bees for their honey. They are cross and fight.

All wasps are not of the same color. There is a wasp of rust-red color. Some are blue-black, some have yellow marks.

LESSON XIV

MRS. WASP'S YEAR

I WILL now tell you of a wasp that does not live alone. This Mrs. Wasp takes good care of her babies. She is called the social wasp.

While it is winter Mrs. Wasp hides. She does not like the cold.

Most wasps die in the winter. Only a few live to come out in the spring.

The first thing Mrs. Wasp does in the spring is to build a new house. She does not use an old house.

She puts her eggs into the house, with some food. When the young wasps grow up, and come out, they help build.

More cells are added to the house. An egg is laid in each cell.

The egg grows into a grub. The wasps feed the grub.

They bring it honey. The baby wasp has no wings or feet.

It has to be shut up, to grow into a true wasp. When the time comes, the wasps put a wax lid upon the cell, and leave the grub to rest.

At last the new wasp eats off the lid, and comes out, a full-grown wasp.

Rooms to Let

Wasps work hard all the time. They fly about for food, and for stuff to make paper, wax, and varnish and glue. They have homes to build, and little wasps to rear.

They seem to know they must nearly all die, when frost comes. When the cold begins, the old wasps look into the cells.

They kill all the eggs, grubs, and half-grown wasps that they find there. Why do they do that?

Do they not seem to love the baby wasps? Yes.

They kill them quickly to keep them from dying of hunger and cold. Is not that an odd way to show love?

Some wise people do not feel sure that the wasps kill the little ones in this way.

Rooms to Let

Do not forget that the wasp does not grow after it gets its wings and leaves its cell. When it comes out, it is full grown.

When it is a fat, round, wingless grub it is called a larva. When it has changed its shape, and has wings, it is called a pupa.

Some call the pupa a nymph. Are those very hard words? Try and keep them in mind.

LESSON XV

MRS. WASP AT HOME

THERE are many kinds of wasps. There are mud wasps, which make mud houses.

Lonely wasps build alone in the ground, and dig holes in the sand. They throw the sand back between their hind legs.

Did you ever see your dog dig a hole? The wasp digs in the same way as the dog does.

Sand wasps make tiny earth houses on walls and fences. Tree wasps hang great paper houses upon the branches or twigs of trees.

Rust-red wasps do not build houses for

their cells. They make fine paper cells, and hang them with the open part down, in some safe place.

They varnish the cells to keep them dry. In a cold land, the wasps build in barns, attics, hollow trees, or in the ground.

In warm lands, they hang a bunch of cells out in the open air, on trees or vines.

One day I found a wasp's nest in an old tin can. There had been paint in the can. The wasp had made a stem of paint.

She used her feet to twist it into a stiff rope. Upon

Rock-a-bye Baby

A Cosy Nest

that, for a stem, she built a nest like a white flower.

She put a cell upon the stem, and six cells around that one. In each cell was a wee, white egg.

The eggs grew to fat grubs. They had black heads.

Then Mrs. Wasp fed them. She went from one cell to the other, and fed her grubs, just as a bird feeds its young.

Mrs. Wasp also makes a pap of bugs and fruit, and gives it to her young.

Wasps are very neat. They keep their

nests clean. They use cells more than once. But they make new nests each year.

One kind of wasp is called the White Face; its face is white.

Every wasp has a clean, shining coat, and a fierce look; but the White Face is the fiercest looking of all.

Wasps do not bite or chew food; they suck out the juices of fruit and insects. They also eat honey.

LESSON XVI

REVIEW

WHERE, and how, does Mr. Crab make his house? Where are Mr. Crab's bones?

Where are yours? Will you tell me how Mr. Crab gets his new coat?

Tell me some of the kinds of crabs that you know of. What do crabs eat?

Why does one kind of crab steal a shell? Tell me about a crab's eyes.

How is the crab made, which likes to swim on the deep sea? What is a sea tide?

How many tides are there each day? How do little crabs grow?

Where do crabs hide, when they are afraid? What animals catch and eat crabs?

Of what use are crabs? Did I tell you that some crabs eat seaweed?

What is a wasp? How many legs and wings has Mrs. Wasp?

How is her body made? Why do her two wings on each side seem one?

Tell me what kind of houses wasps build. What can wasps make?

How do baby wasps grow? Tell me how wasps make paper.

What else do you know about crabs and wasps? What can you say about a wasp's sting?

How does the wasp eat?

LESSON XVII

THE BEE AND THE MAN

DID you ever see a hive of bees? Are you afraid of bees? Do not be afraid of them. They do not often sting those who let them alone. There are some people whom bees never sting.

Do you see how small the bees are? Do they not move very quickly? Are not their cells very small?

Now I will tell you a strange thing. The man who knew most about bees was a blind man! His name was Huber. He lost his sight when he was a boy. He liked to study. Most of all, he liked to study bees.

When he was a boy, he had a friend. She was a kind girl. She, too, loved to study. When she grew up, she became Huber's wife.

Huber was not poor. He had a happy home of his own. He had a man to live with him and wait on him. Huber, and his wife, and the man, would go and sit by the

47

bee-hive. The wife read to Huber all the books that had then been made about bees. Then they would watch the bees, to see if they did the things that were told in books.

When they saw the bees do other things, not noted in books, they told Huber. Then they caught bees, and studied the parts of their bodies. Ask your teacher what kind of a glass they used[7] to see the bee with.

The wife and the man told Huber all that they saw done by the bees. He thought it all over. They watched the bees, year after year.

Huber worked fifteen years. Then he made a great book on bees. He told his wife what to write.

He lived to be very old.

It is both from books, and by your own eyes and thought, that you may learn these things. You must watch if you would know. Give time and work to this study.

---

[7] The inside of a gold watch-case, held at angle 45°, is a good magnifier. The teacher should explain a little about the microscope.

LESSON XVIII

A LOOK AT A BEE

THERE are many kinds of bees. The chief of them all is the hive bee. What does the hive bee make for you to eat?

In each hive there are three kinds of bees. The queen bee is the first. She rules all, and she is the mother of all.

The queen bee does no work. She lays eggs in the cells. The father bee is called the drone. He does no work.

Who, then, builds so many fine cells? Who lays up so much honey? Who feeds the baby bees? The small, quiet, brown work bees do all that.

In each hive there is one queen bee to lay eggs. Also there are the drone bees, who hum and walk about. Then there are more than you can count, of work bees, to do all that is done.

How does a bee grow? Like the wasp, the bee is first an egg. Then it is a grub, or a worm. Then, shut in a cell, it gets legs and wings, and grows into a full-grown bee.

The bee is formed of three parts, as a wasp is; but the body is not so slim. The parts are put close to each other. The bee has six legs, and four wings, and many eyes set close like one.

The bee has many hairs on its legs and body. These fine hairs are its velvet coat.

The body of the bee is made of rings of different sizes and shapes; all insects are ring made.

Part of the mouth is a long tongue. It can roll this up: it uses it to get honey from flowers.

The drone bee has a thick body, a round head, and no sting. The queen bee has a long, slim body. Her wings are small. She can sting: so can the work bee.

The work bee is not so large as the other two, but it has large wings. The work bee must fly far for food or wax. The queen bee stays at home.

LESSON XIX

THE BEE AT HOME

LET us look at a work bee. There are two kinds of work bees. Nurse bees take care of the baby bees. The wax bees build the house.

Let us look well at the wax bee. See its body. Here are the rings, and here are the scales of wax on each ring. The wax is made in the bee from the honey or sweet food that the bee eats.

In the bee's body are two bags. Into one bag it puts the honey that it gets from flowers. It takes this home and puts it into the cells. What goes into the other bag feeds the bee and makes wax.

Look at this bee's legs. On each leg is a basket, a brush, and a tool with which to pinch and press the wax into the cells.

When the bee goes into a flower, it gets covered with pollen-dust. The brush on its legs takes off this dust from the bee's coat and puts it into the basket. That dust is to feed the young bees.

Sweets to the Sweet

With the tool it strips the scales of wax from the rings on its body. Then it takes the wax in its mouth and lays it to build the wall of the cells.

Did you ever see a man lay brick on a wall? The bee builds her walls very much as the man builds his.

When the work bees make cells, they first lay down a thick sheet of wax. Then they build upon this little wax boxes, each with six sides, set close to each other. When the boxes are as deep as they should be, the bees fill them. These boxes are called cells.

Some of the cells are for the dust, or food, called bee-bread. Some cells are for the baby bees to lie in. Some cells are for honey.

The queen puts eggs in all the cells that are for bees. The nurse bees put in flower dust for the baby bees to eat.

The wax bees build the cells and get honey. The wax bees have pockets for wax. The nurse bees have only small pockets or baskets. The queen bee and the drones have no pockets.

LESSON XX

THE BEE BABIES

A BEE does not live more than three or four years.[8] The work bees know that some of the grubs must grow to be queens, others to be drones, and others work bees. They

---

[8] Many bees live but a few weeks. Some claim that the life of a work bee is never longer than six months.

make for the baby queen bee a large, round cell.

In each hive there are five or six cells for these baby queens.

The nurse bees feed the grubs. They give the baby queens all they can eat of very nice food. The grub of the new queen bee grows large, and eats as much as it wants.

The work-bee babies are in small cells. Their food is plain bee-bread. They are fed less than the queen-grubs. Then shut in their tight cells they turn into work bees.

After a time the grubs shut in the big cells turn into queen bees. They begin to sing a song.

The queen bee hears it. She knows that more queen bees will come out.

That makes her angry.

She runs at the cells, to try to kill the new queens. The work bees all stand in her way. They will not let her kill the new queens.

There can be only one queen in a hive at

one time. So the old queen says, "Come! I will go away! I will not live here any more!"

Many of the old bees say, "We will go with our queen." Then they fly out of the hive in a cloud. They wish to find a new home.

Did you ever see bees swarm? They may fly far away, or they may light near by. They hang on a vine, or branch, or

First Flight

stick, like a bunch of grapes. Can you put them into a new hive? Yes, but you must put the queen in, too. They will not live where there is no queen mother.

Drop them softly into a new hive where

there is a piece of honey-comb. In a few hours they are calm. Then they go to work.

The work bees begin to make cells. They spread wax. They build walls.

If a young bee lays a bit of wax wrong, some old one takes it up and lays it right.

LESSON XXI

THE BEE WAR

AFTER the old queen goes out in a rage, what do the rest of the bees do? They all keep still, but they look toward the cells where the new queens sing. Then one new queen breaks off the lid of her cell and comes out.

She lifts her head, spreads her wings, dries her legs. Her legs are like gold. Her dress is velvet and gold. She is fine!

The bees fan her and feed her. But just then a cell near by opens, and out comes one more new queen!

This will not do. Two queens do not live in one hive. When the two queens see each other, they rush together and begin to fight.

Battle Royal

If they stop the fight to rest, the work bees make them keep on. At last one of them stings the other near the wing, and kills her.

Then this strong queen runs to the other cells, where the baby queens lie. She tears off the wax lids and stings each new queen bee. Then it dies.

Now the strong queen is the one true queen of the hive. Her rage is at an end. The bees come to her and touch her.

They are proud of their fine, new queen, and love her. They carry out all the dead bees from the hive, and in great joy build new cells.

The queen bee leaves the hive but twice. A few weeks after she is made queen, the work bees let her go out once into the sun and air. But her wings are very small. She cannot fly far.

She has no bag for dust. She does not need to get honey. All she has to do is to come home and lay eggs.

She does not go out again until the next year. Then she leads off a swarm of old bees, and leaves the hive to the next new queen bee.

LESSON XXII

THE BEE'S WORK

You now know how the new queen bee grows and how she lives. Let us see how the work bee gets on. The work bee in its small cell does not grow so large as the queen bee. It has larger wings. When it is a true bee, it pulls or breaks off the cap of its cell and comes out. It is wet and cold and weak.

Near by is a cell, open, and full of honey. The new bee takes a nice meal. Then it goes out of the hive into the sun.

The other bees come to it, and touch it with their feelers. They lick it with their tongues, to smooth its brown coat, and help it to spread its wings.

Then off it goes to get honey and flower dust. It knows how at once. It does not need to learn.

It finds its way. It knows the right flowers. It tries to keep out of the way of things that will hurt it.

What color do the bees like best? They like blue best, and red and purple next best. They like flowers with a sweet smell, and all flowers that have honey.

They bring home dust of flowers, honey, and a kind of gum. The gum is to line the cells and to help make them strong.

If a queen bee dies, and all the baby queens are also dead, what can the bees do? They take a baby work bee and make a queen.

Can they not live if they have no queen? No, not long; there will be no eggs laid.

How do they make a queen of a work bee? They pick out a good grub. They put it into a round queen cell.

They feed the work grub with the queen-food, or "royal jelly." When it grows up, it is not a work bee, but is a queen.

LESSON XXIII

THE WISE BEES

In the bee-hive all is not peace and joy. Foes come in and try to kill the poor bees.

The Fate of the Intruder

Who are these foes? A caterpillar may come into the hive to live. The bees do not like him. He is not clean; he is in their way.

Slugs also come in. Snails and moths come to steal the honey. When the foe is a small fly or slug, the bees kill it and take it out.

A large worm or a slug they cannot take out. What do they do then? They kill it, if they can, with their stings. Then they build over it a tomb, or grave, of wax and gum.

A Foe at the Gate

That is to keep any bad smell from the cells. If a snail comes in, they take this same strong gum and glue him to the floor. Then he must die in his shell.

If a strange queen flies in, they will not sting her, but she must not stay. So the work bees form a ball about her, until she dies for lack of air.

I have told you how wasps kill bees. Birds eat bees. Some birds break into the hive to get honey. Bears like honey. They break up wild bees' nests.

Hens and toads eat bees. Moths make the worst trouble in bee-hives.

In June or July, the work bees kill all the drones. They do not wish to feed them when it is cold. Bees lay up honey to eat when the flowers are dead and gone.

In the winter, bees sleep most of the time. They need some food to eat when they rouse. As soon as spring comes, they come out and go to work.

LESSON XXIV

EARTH BEES

Do all bees build in hives? No. Wild bees like to build in hollow trees.

In hot lands, some bees build in holes in the rocks. Swarms of bees that leave hives find odd places to live in. I knew of a swarm that found a hole in the roof of a house.

The bees got into the roof and lived there, five years. When a man took them out they had two big tubs full of

A City in a Tree

comb. Is it not odd that bees can make so much wax from their small wax-bags?

Did you ever find in the earth the nest of a humble-bee? The humble-bee queen works. Humble-bees dig holes in the earth with their front feet.

When they have made a hall and a room, they make a nest. It is of grass, or leaves, or hay, cut fine. They lay eggs in the nest.

They make honey in large combs. The combs are more soft and dark than those which the hive bee makes. Field mice and moles eat these bees and their combs.

One little bee, that lives alone, saws out a nest in a post or a tree. She makes one room over the other. In each she puts an egg and food.

She seals up the door with a paste made of sawdust. Then she goes off and dies. The next spring out come the new bees.

They know how to get food and make homes, just as the mother did.

One kind of bee makes a house much like an ant-hill. She makes a long hall. From the hall she opens small rooms. In each room she puts food, in a ball like a pea. Then she lays an egg by it, and leaves the small bee to grow up alone.

LESSON XXV

OTHER BEES

ONE bee is called a mason bee. She takes fine mud or clay, to make a cell. The cell is the shape of an urn. Now and then, she builds this urn in an empty snail shell.

One kind of mason bee is of a dark green color. Mason bees are very small. Some mason bees live in holes in the ground. In the hole they make a clay cell like a box.

They are so neat that they do not like to see a mud wall. What does the bee do to her wall? She cuts out bits of nice, soft leaves, and lines her cell! Some bees take bits of green leaves, as of the plum tree, but they like bright color best. One kind of bee lines her cell with the petals of roses. When she has glued them all over the cell, she then puts into it some food and an egg.

Do you not think the new bee will like its gay, pink cell? One kind of bee likes red poppy leaves best. She cuts the bits of leaf quite small.

There is a bee in Brazil, which makes a large nest, like a great bag. It is full of round balls. The balls are full of honey. The wax and honey of this bee are of a dark color.

One kind of bee has no sting. Would you like that bee best?

The tree bee is also called the wild bee. This bee chooses an old tree with a

Jack of all Trades

hollow trunk. It cleans out more and more of the old, dead wood, and builds nice combs.

A tall tree may be full of combs, from root to top. In such a tree, more than one swarm will live and work. Each swarm has its queen, and keeps in its own place.

Smoke makes bees fall as if dead. People drive bees off with the smoke from a fire of wood or paper.

When I was a little girl, our bees sometimes swarmed on the Fourth of July. I had to stay at home and watch them, and I am sure I did not like that.

LESSON XXVI

MORE ABOUT BEES

WOULD you like to own bees? Once I knew a boy who had some bees. He kept them in a room, at the top of his house. He left the window open, and the bees came and went as they chose.

A swarm of bees costs about five dollars.

Each year it may gain for you five dollars, or more, by honey, and a new swarm.

If you live in the city, you cannot so easily keep bees. Why not?

They could not find the right food.

They need to fly in the field or in a garden, so that they can get the honey and the yellow dust of flowers. They need to fly where they can get the thick gum from trees to line their cells.

If you have a hive of bees, you should learn to watch them well. Like Huber, you may find out some new things. We do not yet know all about bees. We could learn more than is now known about drones.

If you stand by a hive, the bees will not hurt you if you keep still, and do not get in their way to the door as they go in and out.

Bees lay up for winter more honey than they need. So the bee-keepers take out much of it to eat or to sell.

They must leave some for the bees. If too much comb is taken out, the bees must be fed. You can give them sugar or some sweet stuff. Bees like flour made of peas.

They cannot feed the young bees if they do not have sweet dust or flour. They cannot make wax if they have no sweet food. They cannot line their cells, or seal them well, if they have no strong gum from trees.

I know some people who think bees like to hear a song, and so sit near the hives and sing to them. But bees, really, like color, and sweet smell, and nice tastes, and do not care much for any noise.

LESSON XXVII

THE SPIDER AND HIS DRESS

FLIES, wasps, bees, and ants are insects. Insects have six legs, and their bodies have three parts. An insect is at first a tiny egg. From the egg comes a grub, and the grub turns to a full-grown wasp, or fly, or bee, or other insect.

When it first gets its legs and wings, and comes out of its cell or case, it is as large as it ever will be. Insects do not grow after they get wings. The small fly does not grow to be a big fly, nor the small bee to be a big bee. The first size they have when they come out is the size that they keep.

The spider is a creature of another kind. It lays eggs, and out of the eggs come little spiders. They grow to be big ones. The spider changes its size, it grows. It moults its skin, as the crab moults its shell.

A Spider

The body of the insect is hard, and is made in rings. It cannot pull off its coat to get bigger, as a crab can.

The spider's body is soft. Its skin is tough; it changes its skin often when it is very young.

The spider has eight legs instead of six, and most spiders have eight eyes. The spider's body is in two parts. Its poison is not in a sting in the tail. It is in the base of the two jaws.

The spiders are somewhat like crabs;

somewhat like some insects, as the daddy-long-legs. The real daddy-long-legs is a fly with long legs. A spider that has just such legs is also called a daddy-long-legs.

Daddy-long-legs

The front part of the spider's body is not so large as its hind part. The front part has all the eight legs and the head.

The spider has no wings; he has two small front legs, or hands, with five joints. He uses them to feel with, and to take his food.

You will see on the head of the spider two short fangs. They are its jaws. They have the poison in them. They are used to bite.

The claws on the eight feet of a spider are very much like a lion's claws. The claws have a brush of hairs on them.

The spider can walk up a wall. The brush on his feet will not let him drop off. He uses his legs to jump and to walk, and to guide his thread when he spins.

Spiders spin webs. The hind part of the spider is large and round. It has six small, round tubes. Each of these tubes is made of many very small tubes. What are they for? They are to spin this web. What is the web?

In the tube is a kind of glue. When it is drawn out into the air, it gets hard. It is then a fine silk, and as it comes out it is woven into a net which we call a web. All spiders spin webs.

Spiders are of all colors. Their dress is like velvet. It is black, brown, red, and gold. It is in stripes and spots. The spider is like a king in his rich dress.

The eight eyes of the spider cannot move. They are set so that they can see every way at once.

While the spider is growing, he pulls off his dress as Mr. Crab does. The crab's bones are his coat. The spider has no bones, but his skin is hard and tough, and before the baby spiders are two months old, they shed their coats three or four times.

We say they moult when they do this. They spin a bit of line to take firm hold of. Then the skin on the front part of the body first cracks open; then after this the skin on the hind part falls off; and by hard kicks they get their legs free.

The new skin is fine and soft but soon grows firm and tough.

The spider is somewhat like a crab and somewhat like an insect. Look at this table.

Crab	Spider	Insect
8 legs.	8 legs.	6 legs.
No wings.	No wings.	4 wings.
Moults.	Moults.	Never moults.
Lays eggs.	Lays eggs.	Lays eggs.
	Body in 2 parts.	Body in 3 parts.
Shell hard.	Shell tough.	Body hard.
2 eyes.	8 eyes.	Many eyes.

You now see that a spider is nearer to the crab family than to the insects. They are all ring-made creatures; their legs and bodies are made of rings of various sizes, joined together.

LESSON XXVIII

THE SPIDER AT HOME

THE spider is busy all the time. It is not cross like a wasp. The bite of a spider does not do a man or a child much harm. A spider does not bite unless it is hurt, or when it kills its food. It bites to kill flies, bees, ants, and such things, to eat.

Spiders make webs, nets, and snares.

The Child's Swing

They can spin, weave, dig, and hunt. Some can build rafts, and others make mud houses.

Their webs are to live or lie in. They are also to catch insects. The nests are for baby spiders.

The snares are to catch food. The silk of the web is very fine, but it is strong. It will hold up a big, fat spider. It will hold fast a wasp or a bee.

The Spider's Swing

Do you see the spider on his thread? It is his swing. He can swing as the boy does in his rope swing.

Do you see the spider lie at rest in his web?

The Spider at Rest in His Web

Do you see the child rest in a web made of string?

How does the spider make his web?

First he finds a good place. He presses the end of the tube he spins with, and makes a drop of glue fast to a wall, or leaf, or stem. Then he drops away; and as he goes, the glue spins out in many fine streams, which unite into one, and stiffen to silk-like thread. If he does not find a good place to make his web fast, he can climb back!

How can he climb back? He runs up his line as fast as he came down. If you scare

The Child Rests in a Web Made of String

him, he drops down on his line like a flash. It will not break.

If you break it, he gets away quickly. Then he runs off to find a new place to which to make a line fast.

The long lines in the web are called rays. The spider spins the rays first. The rays are spread out like the spokes of a wheel.

The spider guides the lines with his feet as he spins. He pulls each one to see if it is firm. Then he spins a thread, round and round, from ray to ray, until the web is done.

Webs are of many shapes. You often

see the round web spread on the grass on warm mornings. People call them "Ladies' Mantles."

LESSON XXIX

THE LITTLE NEST

THE web of the spider is made of two kinds of silk. The silk of the rays is smooth. The silk that goes across the rays has tiny drops of glue on it. This makes the line stick to the rays.

Mrs. Spider begins her lines at the outer edge. They are laid nearer to each other as she gets to the centre of the web. When all is done, she is in the centre, and does not need to walk on her new web.

She has a nest near her web. From the nest runs a line. Mrs. Spider can sit in the door of her nest, and hold the line in her claw. When a bug or fly goes on the web, the web shakes. She feels her line move. She runs down the line and gets the fly or bug, and takes it to her nest to eat.

Before she takes the prey to her nest, she kills or stuns it. Then she winds some fine web about it. She makes a neat bundle of it, and then carries it off.

You can make Mrs. Spider run down her line if you shake the web a very little with a bit of grass or stick. She will run out to see if she has caught a bee or a fly.

The nest of the spider is made of close, fine silk. It is like soft, nice cloth.

A Snare

In shape it may be like a ball, or a horn, or a basket. Each kind of spider makes its web in the shape it likes best. In the nest the spider lays her eggs in a silk ball. The eggs, at first, are very soft. After a time they grow harder.

More than two spiders never live in a nest. Often a spider lives all alone. Spiders often bite off each other's legs. A spider can live and run when half its legs are gone. It can also get a fine new leg as a crab can. The new leg is smaller than the one lost.

When the baby spiders come out of the egg, they must be fed. The mother takes good care of them.

They grow fast. When they are grown, they go off and make their own webs. Sometimes the eggs are left in the silk ball all winter.

The baby spiders come out in the spring. Then the old ones are dead. But the young ones know how to hunt and to spin. The very young spiders do not have as rich a dress as the old ones. The hairs of their coat are not so thick at first.

The soft, silk-like coat, with its rich color, is the only beauty a spider has. People do not admire his long legs and his round, soft, bag-like body. Still, some people who watch spiders learn to like them very well.

THE SPIDER AND HIS FOOD

SOME people say that they "hate spiders." Why do they dislike them? "Oh," they say, "they are so very greedy!" Well, a spider must eat a great deal, or he cannot spin his web.

His food makes the glue that makes the web. Spiders work hard. So they must eat much.

"But they bite." They will not bite you if you do not hurt them. If they do, the bite will do you no harm. They bite insects to kill them.

Do you not eat fish, meat, and birds? Who kills this food for you?

"But the spider is not pretty." True, his shape is not pretty, nor are his long hairy legs pretty. Just see his fine black or gold coat! Is not that pretty?

If he is not pretty, he is wise and busy. Webs are very pretty, if spiders are not.

Spiders eat flies and all kinds of small bugs. When a fly is fast in a web, he hums loud from fear. He seems to know that the spider will come and eat him.

The spider will eat dead birds. One kind of spider kills small birds to eat.

When spiders eat they do not chew their food; they suck out the juice.

There is a spider that lives on water. He knows how to build a raft.

He takes grass and bits of stick, and ties them up with his

His Diving-bell

82

silk. On this raft he sails out to catch flies and bugs that skim over the water.

There is a spider that lives in the water. She can dive. Her nest is like a ball. It shines like silver. Her web is so thick that it does not get wet. Her velvet coat keeps her as dry as a fur coat. Her eggs are of the color of gold.

Spiders are very neat. They hate dust and soot.

They will not have a dirty web. If you put a bit of dirt or leaf on the web, Mrs. Spider will go and clean it off.

She shakes her web with her foot until all the lines are clean. If the dirt will not shake from the web, the spider will cut the piece out, and mend the web with new lines.

Spiders are great water drinkers. They cannot bear drought. They soon die of thirst.

LESSON XXXI

VERY STRANGE SPIDERS

I HAVE told you of the spider that dives. I also told you of the spider that makes a raft. The one that makes the round web is the garden spider.

There is a spider that runs on water. How can she do that? Have you seen boys dash about on ice with skates on their feet? Did you ever see a man walk on snow-shoes? This spider wears shoes.

They are shoes made for walking on the water. What are they like? They are like bags of air. It is as if she had a wee toy-balloon on each of her eight feet. She cannot sink.

There is one spider called a trap-door spider. She lives in the ground. She digs a tube down, and makes her nest deep in the earth.

Then she makes a door. It is a nice door at the top of the hole. It has a hinge. It will open and shut.

It is like the lid of a box. How does she

make this? She spins a thick, round web. She fills it with earth.

Then she folds the web over, to hold in the dirt. She makes a hinge of web. This trap-door will open and shut. It is firm and strong.

But the odd thing is, that the spider plants moss or small ferns on this door! She digs the moss up, sets it on her door, and it grows well. These trap-door spiders eat ants and worms.

Traps and Snares

When they come out of their holes, they leave the door wide open so that they can go back.

Once a man put a lady-bird at a spider's

trap-door. She took it in to eat. She found it had too hard a shell for her to bite. So she took it back and laid it out by her door.

Then the man put a soft grub by the door, and the spider took that to eat. She did not bring that back. She ate it. Spiders now and then eat other spiders, but not often.

One kind of spider makes a tent of leaves. She ties the leaves down with silk. She lives in the tent and keeps her eggs there.

One garden spider makes a nest in the shape of a pear. One ties a little ball to stems of grass. Two or three stems are tied together to hold the ball firmly.

The young spiders have not their thick coats at first. Small spiders will stay by their mother and sit on her back. They act like the small chicks with the hen. Most spiders live only one year. Some live two. Others live over four.

There are some mason spiders. When a man is a mason, what does he do? In what does he work? There are mason wasps, and mason bees, and mason worms. Mason spiders make nests of clay.

They take the clay in small bits and build a clay mug. It is six inches long. They line it with thick silk. The door is like a box lid. It has a hinge.

Some spiders are so small you can hardly see them. One of the very wee ones is clear, bright red. Some are very big. The big ones are black, with spots and stripes, and have thick coats like fur.

If you could find a tower spider, or a trap-door spider, and sit down to watch it build or catch its food, I think you would be happy for a whole day, or for many days. The tower spider builds over her hole a neat tower two or three inches high; she sits on her tower. She has as many as fifty baby spiders at once. They sit on her back for four or five weeks, until they moult two or three times. They do not fight with each other.

When Mrs. Spider gets a fly or a bug for the little ones to eat, she crushes it, and the baby spiders come and suck the juice, as she holds the food for them.

LESSON XXXII
REVIEW

WHAT is an insect?

Name some kinds of insects.

Can you tell me how an insect's body is made?

How many legs, wings, and eyes do insects have?

What three kinds of bees live in each hive?

Tell me what the queen bee does.

What does a drone bee do, and how does he look?

Which bee makes cells?

How do bees get honey and wax?

Tell me how nurse bees take care of bee babies.

How can nurse bees make a new queen bee?

Why do the queen bees fight?

Tell me about the fight of the queen bees.

Why does a swarm of bees leave the hive?

What do bees eat?

What do they make?

Tell me of odd places where bees live.

What things eat the bees and steal their combs?

How must you take care of bees, if you have them?

What colors do bees like best?

Tell me about ground bees.

Tell me about mason bees.

Do all bees make combs with cells that have six sides?

Is a spider an insect?

In what is he not like insects?

What can a spider make?

How does the spider spin a web?

Tell me about the spider's eyes.

How does a spider tend its young ones?

Tell me about the water spider.

What can you tell about other strange spiders?

What does a spider eat?

What good things can you say for the spider?

LESSON XXXIII

OUT OF HARM'S WAY

By this time I am sure you think that all the small bugs, flies, spiders, and crabs will soon be dead. You have found how cold kills them. You have heard how they kill each other. You know that men and birds and beasts kill them.

How can any live? What is there to save the poor things? The two chief things that save them are their shape and their color. Why, how is that? Let us see how shape and color protect these living things.

On the sand by the sea the crab that lives mostly out in the air is of a gray color. It has fine red spots like sand. The shell of this crab looks so much like sand that, if he lies flat and still, you can scarcely see him.

The crab that lives on the sea-side mud is black-green like the mud. Birds cannot see him very well, he is so like the mud that he lies upon.

The spiders that live in the woods have the color of a dead leaf.

Some of them, as they lie in their webs, fold up their legs and look like a dead leaf. One spider puts a row of dead leaves and moss all along her web. She lies on this row, and looks like part of it. Birds cannot see her, as she lies in this way.

One small bee that lives in trees is green, like a new leaf. The bees, in brown, black, and gold, look like parts of the flowers on which they alight.

Birds and beasts that live in snow lands are often white, as the polar bear and the eider duck.

Snakes that live on trees, or on the ground, are often brown or green. They look like the limbs of trees.

Little lizards in walls are gray like stone. In woods, they often are the color of a dead twig. They can fold up, or stretch out, and look like twigs, or leaves, or balls of grass or hay.

All this will keep them from being seen by animals that would kill them.

Some of them, you know, have hard shells to shield them. Did I not once tell you how fast they move? They dart, and run, and jump, quick as a flash of light. That helps them to get out of the way.

Did I not tell you, also, that the crab has his eyes set on pegs? He can turn them every way to see what is near him.

The insect and the spider do not have their eyes on long pegs. Some kinds have six or eight eyes. These eyes are set in a bunch, and some face one way, some another. They can see all ways at once.

Then, too, so many small live things grow each year, that they cannot all be put out of the way.

Each crab will lay more eggs than fifty hens. One spider has more baby spiders than you can count. One bee has more new bees in the hive each year than there are people in a large city. In a wasp's big nest there are, no doubt, as many wasps as there are leaves on a great tree.

Of the creatures which it is most easy to kill, very many are born. And so, while many of them perish each day, many are left to live.

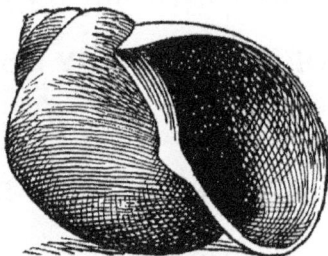

LESSON XXXIV

SHELL-FISH

HAVE you not all heard the song, "Rock-a-by, Baby, in the Tree-top"? What babies live in tree-tops? You will say, "Bird, wasp, bee, and spider babies swing in the trees."

Do you know that there are small cradles that rock all day long on the waves?

Up and down, in the sun, on the water, rock the cradles of many shell-fish.

What are shell-fish?

They are soft sea-animals that live in hard shells.

But you must know that these are not true fish. A true fish is an animal that lives in the water, and has a back-bone. The back-bone of a fish is very much like your back-bone.

All fish can swim. Most of them have fins and scales. Very many of them have long, slim, smooth bodies, that will glide easily through the water.

All of you can see fish, in the ponds, lakes, or brooks near your home. You often have them to eat on your table.

If you live in the city, you can go to the place where fish are sold and look at them. In some other book I may tell you a little about the true fishes.

In this book I shall now tell you a very little about what are called "shell-fish."

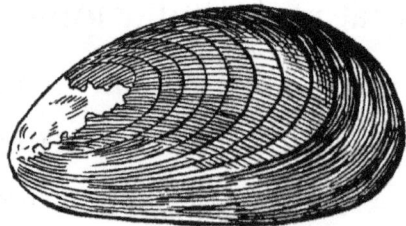

This is not a very good name for them, but we will use it, because you will hear it from many people, and will often see it used in books.

The right name for these shell-fish is a hard word, which means "soft body" or "soft thing." That suits them very well, for they are all soft bodies; they have no bones.

There are also in the water soft-bodied things that have no shells to cover them. In the next book we shall tell you of some of them.

The soft things that live in shells are mostly round or wedge shape. Their shells serve them for houses to live in, for ships to sail in, for coats to cover them, for bones to keep their soft bodies in shape.

The shells of these soft things are of many forms. Some are all in one piece, like a twist or curl. Some have two parts, like the covers of a book. These two parts are held by a hinge. And some shells are made in many pieces or scales.

There are three kinds, or orders, of shell-fish. One kind has a head on its foot. Another has a head much like that of the snail. Still another kind has no head. Well! That *is* a queer thing, to have no head!

Let us learn first about the shell-fish with a head and a foot.

There are many kinds of shell-fish of this order. They differ in size, color, shape, and way of life. But if we learn about one, we shall have an idea of them all.

You know that the hermit crab steals a shell to live in. It is often a long shell, like a curl. That is the sort of shell that shell-fish with heads live in. It is a shell all in one piece.

These shells are very hard and thick. Why is that? The fish in them is soft. It has no bones.

If these soft things had no hard shells, they could not live. The waves would kill them. The crabs, fish, and other animals in the sea, would eat them at once.

Let us see how a shell-fish is made. Have you a shell to look at? If not you can look at these shells in the picture. The conch, or winkle, is the largest shell-fish you will be likely to find. His body is soft but tough. It runs to a point.

That back part takes fast hold of the post in the shell, so that Mr. Conch will not drop out. On one side of his body he has a hook like a thumb. That is to pull him back into his shell when he wishes to hide.

The front end of the conch is wide and thick. Here we find his mouth. Near his mouth he has two feelers, such as insects have, to touch things. Where the feelers join his head he has two eyes.

His foot is flat, and is as big as all the rest of his body. It is just the size of the open part of his shell. Why is that?

The shoe on his foot is hard, like horn. When he draws back into his shell, that shoe is his door. It fits close. It shuts him in safe in his shell.

LESSON XXXV

THE STORY OF MR. CONCH

THE conch, or winkle, does not like to live in sand, or on hard rock. He likes deep water, where he can have some sand and some rock. When the wind blows, and the sea is very rough, he digs his stout foot into the sand near a stone, and holds fast. Then he will not drift on shore.

If he is cast on the shore, he will die. Mr. Conch and his family cannot live out of water. The little ones would be killed by dry wind. Mrs. Conch also likes some soft sand for a bed for her babes in their queer cradles.

Cast Away on an Island

What does Mr. Conch eat? He eats other shell-fish. He likes to eat oysters. How does he get them?

He goes off to the oyster beds.

He likes the nice young oysters. He picks one up with his foot. You see he uses his foot for a hand as well as for a door. He can spread his foot out very wide. It is very, very strong.

When he has the oyster in his grip, he draws his foot close, as you would shut your hand tight. That breaks up the shell of the oyster. Then Mr. Conch sucks up the oyster at his ease.

The men who own oyster beds do not like him, for he eats many oysters.

Mr. Conch lives a great many years. No one can hurt him in his hard house, and he has all he wants to eat.

His shell is the shape of a large pear. It has a little point at the top, and a long end like a stem. The stem end has a groove in it. His shell has a turn or twist in it, three or four times round. It is sand-color, or pale yellow, outside.

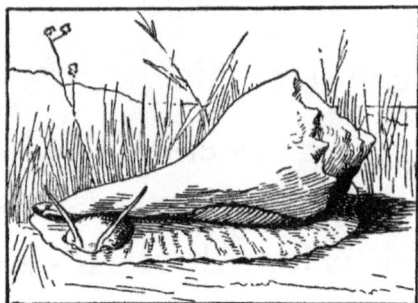

Some shells have dark stripes. Inside, the shell is very smooth, and shines, and is a fine, bright red, or pink, or yellow. It is a very pretty shell.

How does the conch grow? The conch grows from an egg. Most fish lay eggs. So do the shell-fish or mollusks. The eggs of the conch are in a string. They are left lying on the sand to grow.

What is the conch good for? In some places people like them to eat. Fish and crabs eat the conchs' eggs and the young conchs. The shells are made into buttons and breast-pins.

The Indians used to make money from the pink part of these shells. They also used the purple part of the round clam shell for money.

LESSON XXXVI

SEA-BABIES

Now we must learn more about that string of eggs that Mrs. Conch left on the sand. First it was like a thread with knots tied close together on it. Then it grew to be a yard long. It grew very fast.

The knots grew into little cases, or pockets. They were set close to each other. At the ends of the string the cases were small, but after three or four small ones, the others were of the size and shape of big Lima beans.

Once I was out on the sand with a boy.

We found a string of this kind. It had been cast up by the waves. It was of a pale straw-color, and like a long curl.

The boy said, "It is a sea-weed."

I said, "No." Then he said, "It is some kind of a bean or seed." I said, "It is fish seed." Let us look at it.

Each case, or pocket, is flat, and has a rim. The rim has lines in it. In the front edge is a small, round spot, where the case is very thin. This is the door of the case.

Out in the Cold

The sides of the case are very tough. Let us cut one case open. It is full of white gum, or jelly.

I see in it specks like grains of sand. Here is one more string, far up on the sand. This one is dry, hard, and light. The little thin places are real holes now.

The cases are quite empty. Here is one more string. This, too, is light and dry. But the holes in front are not open.

Shake it. Does it rattle? Yes. Cut a case open.

Why! Each case is full of wee shells! Each

shell is as small as a grain of rice! See how thin and white these shells are.

LESSON XXXVII

MORE ABOUT SEA-BABIES

Now in these strings you have the whole story. First, the tiny string Mrs. Conch left on the sand grew to be a big string with large cases like these. The small specks in it were to become shells, and the jelly was to be the food of the baby conchs while in the case. There are very many in each case.

They grew and grew. They ate up all the jelly. They were true shell-fish, only very small. Then it was time for them to go out.

They saw the thin skin over the small, round hole. They felt sure that this was their door. They ate off the thin skin, and went into the sea.

The conch lays its egg-strings from March to May. It lays a great many. In the egg-case the baby shells rock up and down, not on a tree, but on the sea.

This dry string, still full of shells, is one in which the baby conchs are all dead. It was cast on shore when the little ones were too young to come out. That made them all die.

These little things have a hard time to grow up. But if they can live until they are of a good size, they will have a thick shell. Then they will be out of harm's way, and will live a long time.

But how do these shell-fish grow? Do they pull off their shells when they are too tight, as crabs do?

No. All these shell-fish wear a cloak, or veil. It is by their cloak they grow. Why, how is that? This cloak, or veil, is fine and thin. It is part of the body of the fish, and folds all over it.

This fine cloak takes lime out of sea-water, and with it builds more shell. As the animal needs more room, it spreads out this veil over the edge of the shell, and builds with it new shell. You can see the little rims where the cloak built each new piece. The color and the waved lines on the shell are made by this veil.

So the shell-fish need not change his house. He just builds on more room as he wants it.

LESSON XXXVIII

ABOUT MR. DRILL

HERE is a small shell-fish. He looks like Mr. Conch, but he is not so large. He is small. His real size in the sea is not much larger than he is in this picture. His name is Mr. Drill.

His color is dark brown. His shell has ridges on it. The body of the drill is dark green. It has a long tail to twist round in its shell.

The drill does not live alone in a place by himself. A whole host of them live near one another.

The very strangest thing about the drill is his tongue. It is from his tongue that he gets his name.

Did you ever see a man use a file? With it he can cut a hole in a piece of iron or stone. The tongue of the drill is like a file. I wish you could see this queer tongue!

The Little Robber

It is a little soft band that will move in any way, or roll up, or push out. In this fine band are set three rows of teeth. There are many teeth in each row. The teeth are fine and as hard as the point of a pin. We could not see them if we did not use the glass that you were told of.

With this fine tongue the drill can cut or saw a hole in a thick shell.

The drill is very greedy. He eats many kinds of shell-fish. He likes best of all to eat the oyster.

How does he go to work? He cannot break the shell of the oyster as the conch can. No. The way he does is this.

With his tough foot he gets fast hold of the oyster-shell. He picks out the thin, smooth spot called the eye of the shell. Then he goes to work to file his hole. It will take him a long time.

Some say it will take him two days. But he is not lazy. He keeps fast hold and saws away. At last the hole is made clear through the shell.

It is small, smooth, even no man could make a neater hole. Then he puts into the hole a long tube which is on the end of his cloak or veil. He can suck with that, and he sucks up the oyster till the poor thing is all gone.

LESSON XXXIX

THE STORY OF A WAR

WHEN the drill gets on the back of an oyster, what can the oyster do? Nothing. The poor oyster cannot help himself. Does he hear hour after hour the file of the drill on his shell? Yes.

He knows the drill will get in and kill him, but all that he can do is to keep still and wait.

The oyster is not the only kind of shell-fish that the drill eats. When the drill goes after the poor shell-fish that have no heads, he eats them at his ease.

They cannot help themselves. They do not know how to get away from Mr. Drill. The shell-fish that have no heads live in shells made of two parts, like the covers of a book. The two parts are held to each other by a hinge. The oyster has such a shell.

It is a bad thing, it seems, to have no head. Without a head who can take care of himself?

Let us see Mr. Drill try a fight with a shell-fish that has a head. Now he meets his match!

He goes to the top of the shell. He makes fast, and begins—file, file, file. The fish inside hears him. "O, are you there, Mr. Drill?"

Seaside Cottages

What do you think the shell-fish does? He draws his body out of the way, and builds up a nice little wall! So, when Mr. Drill gets his hole made, and puts in his tongue—no fish, only a hard wall! Then Mr. Drill also moves along.

He picks out a good place. Once more he goes to work—file, file, file. "O, *here* you are, Mr. Drill!" And the shell-fish with a head once more pulls his body out of the way, and makes a new wall.

Then Mr. Drill has the same luck as before. Sometimes he gets tired of the war and goes off. Now and then, as he too has a head, he finds a spot where there is no room for the wall. There he makes his hole and sucks out the animal.

You will find very many of the shells on the seabeach with these pinholes in them. The holes were made by Mr. Drill on his hunt for food.

But you will now and then find shells, such as the thick clam shell, full of holes, like a network. This is not done by Mr. Drill.

Shells and bones are made of two kinds of stuff. One is lime, which is hard like stone. The other is not so hard; it is more like dry glue.

These shells with so many holes are old shells, long empty, and the glue part has gone out of them.

How did it get out? It was bored out by a kind of sponge. Only the lime part is left, like a fine net.

When bones or shells have only the lime part left, they will break and crack like glass. If they have too little lime, they will bend.

For all Mr. Drill has a head, he is not so wise as at first he seemed to be.

He will sit down and make a hole in an old dead shell where no fish lives. Now and then he makes a hole in an old shell, long ago turned into stone. He will spend two days on such a shell as this!

Did you know that bones and shells and plants sometimes turn to stone?

You will some day learn about that strange fact.

LESSON XL

HOW SHELL-FISH FEED

Do all the shell-fish feed on other shell-fish? Oh, no. Some of them live on seaweed. Some of them live by fishing. They catch, from the water, small bits of food, as small as grains of sand.

The shell-fish that lives on seaweed has a long, slim tongue. It is somewhat like that of the drill. The tongue is like a tiny strap.

The teeth are set on it, three or more in a row, like the points of pins. As the teeth wear out from work on the tough weed, more grow.

These shell-fish walk along on their one big foot. First one side of the foot spreads out, and then the other.

That pulls them along. Is it not very slow

work? But what of that? All they have to do is to move about and find food. They can take all day for it. They have no houses to build and no clothes to make.

They creep along to a good bed of seaweed. Then they put out the fine, file-like tongue.

At Low Tide

It cuts off flakes of seaweed for them to eat. They are never tired of that one kind of food.

That queer limpet, who sits on a rock and has a shell like a cap, has a head, and a foot, and a tongue that is like a rasp. And he can walk along the floor of the sea.

He can climb up the rocks. The limpet

has his own rock and his own hole in the rock. He goes back to his rock when he has had all that he wants to eat.

The world of the sea is as full of life as the world of the land. There is one nice little shell-fish, not so big as a pea. He lives in the seaweed that grows on rocks. He is brown, or green, or black, or red, or dark yellow.

At Low Tide

He can live in the damp weed in the hours when the tide is out, and has left the rocks dry. He eats seaweed. Let us look at him. He has two little feelers.

He has two wee, black eyes. He has a little

snout, like a tiny pig. At the end of this snout is his little mouth. His small, dark foot has a dent in it.

He puts out his fine, file-like tongue, and laps it out and in, as a dog does when he drinks water. The sharp teeth cut off little scales of weed for him to eat. Take ten or more of these little shells in your hand. Each tiny animal draws in his tiny foot.

As the little animals hide in this way, put down your ear, and you will hear a faint squeak. It is made by the air in the shells.

LESSON XLI

REVIEW

WHAT is a shell-fish?

What three great orders of shell-fish are there?

Are there many kinds?

Name some of the kinds.

What kind of shell do the fish with a head and a foot live in?

Tell me how these shell-fish grow.

Tell me about the conch cradles.

Where do these fish like to live?

Why do they need to wear these hard shells?

Do they change their shells?

How, then, do they grow?

Why are not more blown ashore?

Tell me what they eat.

How do they kill and eat other shell-fish?

Do all fish lay eggs?

How do shell-fish eat seaweed?

What are shell-fish good for?

What shell-fish is most eaten?

What did the Indians make out of the shells?

Tell me about the veil, or cloak, of the shell-fish.

Tell me more about the foot.

Tell me how Mr. Drill makes war.

Of what are shells and bones made?

Describe Mr. Drill's tongue.

www.ingramcontent.com/pod-product-compliance
Lightning Source LLC
La Vergne TN
LVHW090046090426
835511LV00031B/345